Pillars of the Gospel

A Companion Study Guide for
Feast Days for the Contemporary Mind

By Craig Martin Barnes

TEACH Services, Inc.
PUBLISHING
www.TEACHServices.com • (800) 367-1844

Copyright © 2014 Craig Martin Barnes
ISBN-13: 978-1-4796-0135-6 (Paperback)
ISBN-13: 978-1-4796-0136-3 (ePub)
ISBN-13: 978-1-4796-0137-0 (Mobi)

Published by

TEACH Services, Inc.
P U B L I S H I N G
www.TEACHServices.com • (800) 367-1844

Table of Contents

Introduction

All things of the gospel should be understood and interpreted within the framework of this book, which outlines the pillars of the gospel. These "pillars" are not to be confused with the "landmarks," which are 1) the temple of God in heaven and the ark containing the law of God, 2) the light of the Sabbath of the fourth commandment, and 3) the non-immortality of the wicked (Ellen G. White, *1888 Materials*, p. 518).

Please note: Within this book, unless otherwise stated, all emphasis is supplied.

All Bible quotes not otherwise identified, are from the King James Version.

God's Creative Word

God's word has inherent within it the power to create what it says, instantly. Genesis clearly documents the Creation story and how God spoke and formed the universe out of nothing. Jesus Christ is the Creator and the power behind Creation. God calls those things that are not as though they were because they *become real* by His very *speaking* it. God is forever faithful and true—He can never possibly lie, because His word creates the thing that He says.

In the beginning God created the heaven and the earth. And the earth was without form, and void; and darkness was upon the face of the deep. And the Spirit of God moved upon the face of the waters. And God *said*, Let there be light: and there was light. And God saw the light, that it was good: and God divided the light from the darkness. And God *called* the light Day, and the darkness he called Night. And the evening and the morning were the first day.

And God *said*, Let there be a firmament in the midst of the waters, and let it divide the waters from the waters … and it was so. And God *called* the firmament Heaven. And the evening and the morning were the second day.

And God *said*, Let the waters under the heaven be gathered together unto one place, and let the dry land appear: and it was so. And God *called* the dry land Earth; and the gathering together of the waters called he Seas: and God saw that it was good. And God *said*, Let the earth bring forth grass, the herb yielding seed, and the fruit tree yielding fruit after his kind, whose seed is in itself, upon the earth: and it was so … And the evening and the morning were the third day.

And God *said*, Let there be lights in the firmament of the heaven … and it was so.… And the evening and the morning were the fourth day.

And God *said*, Let the waters bring forth abundantly the moving creature that hath life, and fowl that may fly above the earth in the open firmament of heaven.… And the evening and the morning were the fifth day.

And God *said*, Let the earth bring forth the living creature after his kind, cattle, and creeping thing, and beast of the earth after his kind: and it was so.… And God *said*, Let us make man in our image, after our likeness: … So God created man in his own image, in the image of God created he him; male and female created he them.… And God *said*, Behold, I have given you every herb bearing seed, which is upon the face of all the earth, and every tree, in the which is the fruit of a tree yielding seed; to you it shall be for meat. And to every beast of the earth, and to every fowl of the air, and to every thing that creepeth upon the earth, wherein there is life, I have given every green herb for meat: and it was so. *And God saw every thing that he had made, and, behold, it was very good.* And the evening and the morning were the sixth day. (Gen. 1:1–31)

By the *word* of the Lord[1] were the heavens made; and all the host of them by the breath of his mouth. He gathereth the waters of the sea together as an heap: he layeth up the depth in storehouses. Let all the earth fear the Lord: let all the inhabitants of the world stand in awe of him. For he *spake*, and it was done; he commanded, and it stood fast. (Ps. 33:6–9)

In the beginning was the *Word*, and the *Word* was with God, and the *Word* was God. The same was in the beginning with God. All things were made by him; and without him was not any thing made that was made…. And the *Word* was made *flesh* [Jesus Christ], and dwelt among us, (and we beheld his glory, the glory as of the only begotten of the Father,) full of grace and truth. (John 1:1–3, 14)

And to make all men see what is the fellowship of the mystery, which from the beginning of the world hath been hid in God, who created all things by Jesus Christ. (Eph. 3:9)

Through faith we understand that the worlds were framed by the *word* of God, so that things which are seen were not made of things which do appear. (Heb. 11:3)

(As it is written, I have made thee a father of many nations,) before him whom he believed, even God, who quickeneth the dead, and *calleth* those things which be not as though they were. (Rom. 4:17)

For when God made *promise* to Abraham, because he could swear by no greater, he sware by himself, Saying, Surely blessing I will bless thee, and multiplying I will multiply thee. And so, after he had patiently endured, he obtained the promise. For men verily swear by the greater: and an oath for confirmation is to them an end of all strife. Wherein God, willing more abundantly to shew unto the heirs of promise the immutability of his counsel, confirmed it by an *oath*: That by two immutable things, *in which it was impossible for God to lie* [because when He speaks, He creates], we

---

1   This is Yahweh, Jehovah, who is Jesus Christ.

might have a strong consolation, who have fled for refuge to lay hold upon the hope set before us. (Heb. 6:13–18)

As the will of man co-operates with the will of God, it [the will of man] becomes omnipotent. Whatever is to be done at His command may be accomplished in His strength. All His biddings are enablings. (Ellen G. White, *Christ's Object Lessons*, p. 333)

Thus it was that "by the *word* of the LORD" all things were created. He spoke the word only, and it was so: the word *spoken*, itself produced the *thing*.

Thus it was in creation. And thus it was in redemption: he healed the sick, he cast out devils, he stilled the tempest, he cleansed the lepers, he raised the dead, he forgave sins, all by *his word*. In this, also, "he *spake*, and it *was*."

And so he is the same yesterday, and today, and forever. Always he is the Creator. And always he does all things *by his word* only. And always he *can* do all things by his word; because it is the very characteristic of the word of *God*, that it is possessed of the divine power by which itself accomplishes the thing which is spoken.

This is why it is that *faith* is the *knowing* that in the word of God there is this power, the *expecting* the word itself to do the thing spoken, and the *depending* upon that word itself to do that which the word speaks. (A. T. Jones, *Lessons on Faith*, p. 18, emphasis original)

What This Means to Us

God's covenant is His promise, spoken by His creative word. Paul equates the two terms in Galatians 3:14–18. Ellen White and E. J. Waggoner also speak about God's covenant and His promise.

The covenant of grace was first made with man in Eden, when after the Fall there was given a divine promise that the seed of the woman should bruise the serpent's head…. Thus the patriarchs received the hope of salvation.

This same covenant was renewed to Abraham in the promise, "In thy seed shall all the nations of the earth be blessed." Genesis 22:18. This promise pointed to Christ. So Abraham understood it (see Galatians 3:8, 16), and he trusted in Christ for the forgiveness of sins. It was this faith that was accounted unto him for righteousness. (Ellen G. White, *Patriarchs and Prophets*, p. 370)

The covenant and promise of God are one and the same. This is clearly seen from Galatians 3:17, where Paul asserts that to disannul the covenant would be to make void the promise. In Genesis 17 we read that God made a *covenant* with Abraham to give him the land of Canaan for an everlasting possession. Galatians 3:18 says that God gave it to him by *promise*. God's covenants with men can be nothing else than promises to them: "Who hath first given to Him, and it shall be recompensed unto him again? For of Him, and through Him, and to Him, are all things." Romans 11:35, 36, KJV. (E. J. Waggoner, *The Glad Tidings*, p. 71, emphasis original)

Christ forgave the entire human race on the cross. In Luke 23:34 we read, "Father, forgive them; for they know not what they do."

> Jesus prayed for His enemies—"Father, forgive them; for they know not what they do." Luke 23:34. That prayer of Christ for His enemies embraced the world, taking in every sinner who should live, until the end of time. (Ellen G. White, *Story of Redemption*, p. 222)

Our job is to rest in His promise, to *believe* that His word *alone can* do what it says, to *expect* that His word *alone will* do what it says, and to *depend* on His word *alone to do* what it says in us, without our help.

- Matthew 5:48 – God speaks righteousness into us.
- John 8:10–12 – Jesus speaks righteousness into the woman caught in adultery.
- Matthew 8:5–13 – Jesus heals the centurion's servant with the spoken word alone, thus speaking righteousness into the servant.

The Sabbath reminds us of the power of God's creative word. Our job is to *rest* in *His* power and *His* will, not ours.

> Thus the heavens and the earth were finished, and all the host of them. And on the seventh day God ended his work which he had made; and he rested on the seventh day from all his work which he had made. And God blessed the seventh day, and sanctified it: because that in it he had rested from all his work which God created and made. (Gen. 2:1–3)

> And God spake all these words, saying, I am the LORD thy God, which have brought thee out of the land of Egypt, out of the house of bondage. (Exod. 20:1, 2)

> Remember the sabbath day, to keep it holy. Six days shalt thou labour, and do all thy work: But the seventh day is the sabbath of the LORD thy God: in it thou shalt not do any work, thou, nor thy son, nor thy daughter, thy manservant, nor thy maidservant, nor thy cattle, nor thy stranger that is within thy gates: For in six days the LORD made

heaven and earth, the sea, and all that in them is, and rested the seventh day: wherefore the Lord blessed the sabbath day, and hallowed it. (Exod. 20:8–11)

Christis Our Representative

The whole human race was created in Adam, and the whole human race fell because of Adam's sin. This makes Adam the father and the first human representative of the human race. Jesus Christ also represented the human race as its Creator. However, when Adam sinned, the original creation was altered, and if Jesus was going to represent the race in its new, fallen form, He then had to re-qualify by moving to our "district." He had to become a human being and live where we live. This is how Christ could come to this earth as the representative of the human race and be tempted in all points as we are and gain the victory over all areas of sin.

All this solidarity is illustrated when God tells us that two nations are considered to be in Rebecca and that Levi (the father representative of the tribe of priests) paid tithes as did his great-grandfather Abraham, when Abraham paid tithes to Melchisedec.

As the second Adam, Christ took back and reversed all that Adam had lost, and more. As the second Adam representative of the human race, Christ took the judgment of the human race upon Himself so that through His death we could die in Him and through His life we might live in Him and He in us when we believe. This is how we may have life. He shed His blood for every person—past, present, and future—as their representative. Individually, we choose whether to identify with Christ, and be "in Him," or to reject the gift of His representation. This is the "in Christ" concept that Paul writes so much about in his letters.

At His resurrection Christ was the firstfruits of the entire human race in righteousness. And now He ministers for us in the Most Holy Place in the heavenly sanctuary where He is removing the sins from the experience of His people. God holds nothing against us because Christ represents us before the Father. God only sees Jesus Christ, our representative, who is perfect. Thus, we receive all the spiritual blessings that are due to Christ. When we believe His promise to us, then He has our permission to give us the experience of His perfection, actual good works of God in our lives.

Acts 17:24–26 indicates the corporate solidarity of the human race: "God that made the world and all things therein, seeing that he is Lord of heaven and earth, dwelleth not in temples made with hands; Neither is worshipped with men's hands, as though he needed any thing, seeing he giveth to all life, and breath, and all things; And hath made of *one blood all nations of men* for to dwell on all the face of the earth, and hath determined the times before appointed, and the bounds of their habitation."

And the LORD God formed man of the dust of the ground, and breathed into his nostrils the breath of *life* [Hebrew: lives, all lives, including you and me]; and *man*

[Hebrew: mankind, corporately; as well as Adam himself, individually] became a living soul. (Gen. 2:7)

And the LORD said unto her, Two nations are in thy womb, and two manner of people shall be separated from thy bowels; and the one people shall be stronger than the other people; and the elder shall serve the younger. (Gen. 25:23)

And as I may so say, Levi also, who receiveth tithes, payed tithes in Abraham. For he was yet in the loins of his father, when Melchisedec met him. (Heb. 7:9, 10)

For if the firstfruit be holy, the lump is also holy: and if the root be holy, so are the branches. [The firstfruit represents the whole. The firstfruit is to the lump as the root is to the branches.] (Rom. 11:16)

If in this life only we have hope in Christ, we are of all men most miserable. But now is Christ risen from the dead, and become the firstfruits of them that slept. For since by man [mankind, Adam] came death, by man [Christ representing mankind] came also the resurrection of the dead. For as in Adam *all* die, even so in Christ shall *all* be made alive. But every man in his own order: Christ the firstfruits; afterward they that are Christ's at his coming. [Christ is the firstfruits in death and the resurrection, and also the translation of the living when Jesus comes, which covers everyone.] (1 Cor. 15:19–23)

I am the true vine, and my Father is the husbandman. Every branch in me that beareth not fruit he taketh away: and every branch that beareth fruit, he purgeth it, that it may bring forth more fruit. Now ye are clean through the word which I have spoken unto you. *Abide in me, and I in you.* As the branch cannot bear fruit of itself, except it abide in the vine; no more can ye, except ye abide in me. I am the vine, ye are the branches: *He that abideth in me, and I in him, the same bringeth forth much fruit: for without me ye can do nothing.* If a man abide not in me, he is cast forth as a branch, and is withered; and men gather them, and cast them into the fire, and they are burned. If ye abide in me, and my words abide in you, ye shall ask what ye will, and it shall be done unto you. Herein is my Father glorified, that ye bear much fruit; so shall ye be my disciples. [Christ is the firstfruits in life and righteousness, which covers all who believe His promise, His creative word.] (John 15:1–8)

Blessed be the God and Father of our Lord Jesus Christ, who hath blessed us with all spiritual blessings in heavenly places *in Christ:* According as he hath chosen us *in him* before the foundation of the world, that we should be holy and without blame before him in love: Having predestinated us unto the adoption of children by Jesus Christ to himself, according to the good pleasure of his will, To the praise of the glory of his grace, wherein he hath made us accepted in the beloved. (Eph. 1:3–6)

And all things are of God, who hath *reconciled us to himself by Jesus Christ*, and hath given to us the ministry of reconciliation; To wit, that God was in Christ, reconciling the world unto himself, *not imputing their trespasses unto them*; and hath committed unto us the word of reconciliation. Now then we are ambassadors [witnesses] for Christ [in God's trial], as though God did beseech you by us: we pray you in Christ's stead, be ye reconciled to God. *For he hath made him to be sin for us, who knew no sin; that we might be made the righteousness of God in him.* (2 Cor. 5:18–21)

For if, when we were enemies, we were reconciled to God by *the death of his Son*, much more, being reconciled, we shall be saved by his life. (Rom. 5:10)

And Jesus being full of the Holy Ghost returned from Jordan, and was led by the Spirit into the wilderness, Being forty days tempted of the devil. And in those days he did eat nothing: and when they were ended, he afterward hungered. And the devil said unto him, If thou be the Son of God, command this stone that it be made bread. And Jesus answered him, saying, It is written, That man shall not live by bread alone, but by every word of God.

And the devil, taking him up into an high mountain, shewed unto him all the kingdoms of the world in a moment of time. And the devil said unto him, All this power will I give thee, and the glory of them: for that is delivered unto me; and to whomsoever I will I give it. If thou therefore wilt worship me, all shall be thine. And Jesus answered and said unto him, Get thee behind me, Satan: for it is written, Thou shalt worship the Lord thy God, and him only shalt thou serve.

And he brought him to Jerusalem, and set him on a pinnacle of the temple, and said unto him, If thou be the Son of God, cast thyself down from hence: For it is written, He shall give his angels charge over thee, to keep thee: And in their hands they shall bear thee up, lest at any time thou dash thy foot against a stone. And Jesus answering said unto him, It is said, Thou shalt not tempt the Lord thy God. And when the devil had ended all the temptation, he departed from him for a season. And Jesus returned in the power of the Spirit into Galilee: and there went out a fame of him through all the region round about. [By gaining the victory over Satan on all three major points of sin, appetite (lust of the flesh), greed (lust of the eyes), and presumption (pride of life), Jesus Christ, as the representative of the human race, gained for all people victory over all sin. These three categories represent all the sin that is in the world.] (Luke 4:1–14)

Love not the world, neither the things that are in the world. If any man love the world, the love of the Father is not in him. For all [the sin] that is in the world, the lust of the flesh, and the lust of the eyes, and the pride of life, is not of the Father, but is of the world. And the world passeth away, and the lust thereof: but he that doeth the will of God abideth for ever. (1 John 2:15–17)

What This Means to Us

Jesus Christ, as the representative of the human race, conquered sin (and Satan) in our behalf and gave this victory to us as our heritage. He did this through the sinless righteous life that He lived in the same fallen sinful human flesh that we all have. This gift of Christ's righteousness is bequeathed to each of us as an inheritance.

And the word that was spoken to Jesus at the Jordan, "This is My beloved Son, in whom I am well pleased," *embraces humanity*. God spoke to Jesus as our *representative*. With all our sins and weaknesses, we are not cast aside as worthless. "He hath made us accepted in the Beloved." Ephesians 1:6. (Ellen G. White, *The Desire of Ages*, p. 113)

I will be your representative in heaven. The Father beholds not your faulty character, but He sees you as clothed in My perfection. (Ellen G. White, *The Desire of Ages*, p. 357, quoting Christ)

Although Jesus Christ has passed into the heavens, there is still a living chain binding His believing ones to His own heart of infinite love. The most lowly and weak are bound by a chain of sympathy closely to His heart. *He never forgets that He is our representative, that He bears our nature*….

But exalted "to be a Prince and a Saviour, to give repentance to Israel, and remission of sins," will Christ, our representative and head, close His heart, or withdraw His hand, or falsify His promise? No; never, never. (Ellen G. White, *Testimonies to Ministers and Gospel Workers*, pp. 19, 20)

All men have been bought with this infinite price. By pouring the whole treasury of heaven into this world, by giving us in Christ [i.e., as our representative] all heaven,

God has purchased the will, the affections, the mind, the soul, of *every human being*. Whether believers or unbelievers, all men are the Lord's property. (Ellen G. White, *Christ's Object Lessons*, p. 326)

The resurrection and ascension of our Lord is a sure evidence of the triumph of the saints of God over death and the grave, and a pledge that heaven is open to those who wash their robes of character and make them white in the blood of the Lamb. *Jesus ascended to the Father as a representative of the human race*, and God will bring those who reflect His image to behold and share with Him His glory. (Ellen G. White, *Testimonies for the Church*, vol. 9, p. 286)

The whole universe is given to us in Christ, and the fullness of the power that is in it is ours for the overcoming of sin. [More than merely a temporal blessing, it is righteousness, a spiritual blessing.] God counts each soul as of as much value as all creation. Christ has, by grace tasted death for every man, so that every man in the world has received the "inexpressible gift." Hebrew [sic] 2:9; 2 Corinthians 9:15. [Every man, therefore, must be "in Christ" at some point.] "The grace of God, and the gift by grace, which is by one Man, Jesus Christ, hath abounded unto many," even to all; for "as by the offense of one judgment came upon all men to condemnation; even so by the righteousness of One the free gift came upon all men unto justification of life." Romans 5:15, 18, KJV.

Christ is given to every man, each person gets the whole of Him.… *The love of God embraces the whole world, but it also singles out each individual.* [Therefore, what is given to the world as a whole also accrues to each individual.] A mother's love is not divided among her children, so that each one receives only a third, a fourth, or a fifth of it; each child is the object of all her affection. How much more so with the God whose love is more perfect than any mother's! Isaiah 49:15. Christ is the light of the world, the Sun of Righteousness. But light is not divided among a crowd of people. If a room full of people be brilliantly lighted, each individual gets the benefit of all the light, just as much as though he were alone in the room. [All individuals are predestined to be saved in the end (Eph. 3:4–8). If we are not saved in the end, it is because we have chosen to throw away our birthright possession.] *So the life of Christ lights every man that comes into the world.* [The "inexpressible gift" has been given to every person.] *In every believing heart Christ dwells in His fullness.* [When the individual believes, the inexpressible gift already given begins to be seen in the individual's experience.] Sow a seed in the ground and you get many seeds, each one having as much as the original one sown.…

All this deliverance is "according to the will of our God and Father." The will of God is our sanctification. 1 Thessalonians 4:3. *He wills that all men should be saved and come to the knowledge of the truth.* 1 Timothy 2:4. And He "accomplishes all things according to the counsel of His will." Ephesians 1:11. "Do you mean to teach universal salvation?" someone may ask. We mean to teach just what the Word of God teaches—that "the grace of God hath appeared, bringing salvation to all men." Titus 2:11. R.V. God has wrought out salvation for every man, *and has given it to him*; but the majority spurn it and throw it away. The Judgment will reveal the fact that full *salvation* [spiritual blessings as well as temporal] was given to *every* man and that the lost have deliberately thrown away their birthright possession. (E. J. Waggoner, *The Glad Tidings*, pp. 11–14)

Adam satisfied the qualification to represent the human race because he was the father of it. He had, created in him by God, the entire human race, of which he was the first ("firstfruits"). Even Eve came out of Adam, albeit from his rib rather than from his loins.[1] Therefore, because of their sin, we all have Adam's (and Eve's) sin in us. Adam's sin is our sin. Not all of us commit sin in the same way Adam did, nor do we commit sin in the same way as each other do, but deep down inside of each of us is the capability to commit all sin that has ever been committed on the face of the planet. Consequently, no one is better than anyone else. It would be well to *feel* repentance on behalf of others, for you and I are capable of doing the same things. There is a word for this. It is called "corporate repentance."

As we see souls out of Christ, we are to put ourselves in their place, and in their behalf *feel* repentance before God, resting not until we bring them to repentance. If we do everything we can for them, and yet they do not repent, the sin lies at their door; but we are still to feel sorrow of heart because of their condition, showing them how to repent, and trying to lead them step by step to Jesus Christ (Manuscript 92, 1901). (Ellen G. White, *Seventh-day Adventist Bible Commentary*, vol. 7, p. 960)

The Sabbath reminds us that Christ qualified to represent the human race before sin entered because He is the One who created the human race (with His mouth, by the way). He could represent the human race as the Creator of it (John 1:1–14).

After sin entered the world, the human race was no longer as God had created it. Christ had to take fallen sinful human flesh upon Himself in order to qualify to be our representative. He had to become one of us to be a true representative (see Heb. 2:14–18).

---

1   Just as Genesis 2:7 tells us how man came together at Creation, it also implies how humans come apart in death. The body returns to dust, the breath (spirit) returns to God, and the mind (soul) returns to its unconscious state, as it was in Adam before creation, and in you and me before conception, to await the resurrection. See Ecclesiastes 9:4–6; 12:7.

It would have been an almost infinite humiliation for the Son of God to take man's nature, even when Adam stood in his innocence in Eden. But Jesus accepted humanity when the race had been weakened by four thousand years of sin. Like every child of Adam He accepted the results of the working of the great law of heredity. (Ellen G. White, *The Desire of Ages*, p. 49)

Notwithstanding that the sins of a guilty world were laid upon Christ, notwithstanding the humiliation of taking upon Himself our fallen nature, the voice from heaven declared Him to be the Son of the Eternal. (Ellen G. White, *The Desire of Ages*, p. 112)

Satan had pointed to Adam's sin as proof that God's law was unjust, and could not be obeyed. In our humanity, Christ was to redeem Adam's failure…. For four thousand years the race had been decreasing in physical strength, in mental power, and in moral worth; and Christ took upon Him the infirmities of degenerate humanity. Only thus could He rescue man from the lowest depths of his degradation. (Ellen G. White, *The Desire of Ages*, p. 117)

But as He was made of a woman,—not of a man; as He was made of the one by whom sin entered in its very origin into the world, and not made of the man, who entered into the sin after the sin had entered into the world,—this demonstrates beyond all possibility of fair question that between Christ and sin in this world, and between Christ and human nature as it is under sin in the world, there is no kind of separation, even to the shadow of a single degree. He was made flesh; He was made to be sin. He was made flesh as flesh is, and only as flesh is in this world: and was made to be sin only as sin is.

And this must He do to redeem lost mankind. For Him to be separated a single degree, or a shadow of a single degree, in any sense, from the nature of those whom He came to redeem, would be only to miss everything.

Therefore, as He was made "under the law," *because they are under the law* whom He would redeem; and as He was made a curse, *because they are under the curse* whom He would redeem; and as He was made sin, *because they are sinners*, "sold under sin," whom He would redeem,—precisely so He must be made flesh, and "the *same*" flesh and blood, *because they are flesh* and blood whom He would redeem; and must be made "of a woman," *because* sin was in the world *first* by and in the woman.

Consequently, it is true, without any sort of exception,[2] that "*in all things* it behooved Him to be made like unto His brethren." Heb. 2:17.

If He were not of the same flesh as are those whom He came to redeem, then there is no sort of use of His being made flesh at all. (A. T. Jones, *The Consecrated Way to Christian Perfection*, pp. 27, 28, emphasis original)

One more point, and then we can learn the entire lesson that we should learn from the fact that "the Word was made flesh, and dwelt among us." How was it that Christ could be thus "compassed with infirmity" (Heb. 5:2), and still know no sin? Some may have thought, while reading thus far, that we were depreciating the character of Jesus, by bringing him down to the level of sinful man. On the contrary, we are simply exalting the "Divine power" of our blessed Saviour, who Himself voluntarily descended to the level of sinful man, in order that He might exalt man to His own spotless purity, which He retained under the most adverse circumstances. His humanity only veiled His Divine nature, by which He was inseparably connected with the invisible God, and which was more than able successfully resist the weaknesses of the flesh. There was in His whole life a struggle. The flesh, moved upon by the enemy of all righteousness, would tend to sin, yet His Divine nature[3] never for a moment harbored an evil desire, nor did His Divine power for a moment waver. Having suffered in the flesh all that men can possibly suffer, He returned to the throne of the Father as spotless as when He left the courts of glory. When He lay in the tomb, under the power of death, "it was impossible that He should be holden of it," because He "knew no sin." (E. J. Waggoner, *Christ and His Righteousness,* pp. 28, 29)

---

2   This lack of exception is regarding the *flesh*. Christ was different in only one respect—He was born with a sinless *mind*. Christ's sinless mind *could* have sinned as Adam's sinless mind *did* sin, but *not once* did Jesus' sinless mind *ever* consent to the temptations of the fallen sinful human flesh. We, on the other hand, are born with the fallen sinful human mind that will *always* eventually consent to the temptations of the fallen sinful human flesh. What we need is a *change of mind* so that we can be controlled by the sinless mind of Christ (Phil. 2:5). Then we become "partakers of the divine nature" (2 Peter 1:3, 4). (See also A. T. Jones, *General Conference Bulletin 1895*, sermon 17, p. 327.)

3   That is, His divine *mind*.

Pillar #3

Title and Possession

God gave us all things by inheritance as a birthright. He set up a trust fund (in *title*) for each of us before the foundation of the world. At some point in our lives, maybe even at a very young age, God presents Himself to us.[1] If we believe (i.e., say yes), God continues to credit us (in title) with His righteousness (Rom. 4). In addition, we then (through believing) begin to receive the *possession* of these things (in our *experience*). If we *refuse* to believe, thus rejecting Him and throwing away the birthright possession, we do *not* receive the possession (experience) of the righteousness already given to us in title.

Should we ever commit the unpardonable sin, we then lose even our title to the inheritance. This latter decision is irreversible, so don't even come close to doing that. Not to worry, however, for if you have any concern whatsoever about your salvation, you have *not* committed the unpardonable sin (see Matt. 21:28–32).

We are all saved by the death of Jesus Christ. That gift becomes special when we receive the experience (good works) of that salvation through our belief in Jesus. However, in the meantime, because of that salvation given by His death, the whole human race, corporately, sits together in heavenly places (even the Most Holy Place) in Jesus Christ, who is our representative.

When we believe Jesus' gift of salvation, we are accepting our inheritance in the kingdom of heaven, including the heritage of good works that were prepared in advance for us in the perfect life Jesus lived in fallen sinful human flesh as our representative, which we receive daily, as our needs require, and finally when Jesus comes. When we believe, through faith in His promise, Christ dwells in us through the power of the Holy Spirit, and we experience the righteousness that God has given us in title.

This is the "dispensation" that Paul writes about. It is dispensing the assets of the trust fund God has set up for each of us. And the presence of the Holy Spirit in those who believe is the earnest of our inheritance, securing our heritage until Jesus comes and redeems us.

> This is a faithful saying and worthy of all acceptation. For therefore we both labour and suffer reproach, because we trust in the living God, who is the Saviour of all men, specially of those that believe. (1 Tim. 4:9, 10)

> But God, who is rich in mercy, for his great love wherewith he loved us, Even when we were dead in sins, hath quickened us together with Christ, (by grace ye are saved;)

---

[1] Prior to the moment of God presenting Himself to us personally and causing us to have to make a decision, He imputes (credits) righteousness to us, for God winks at our ignorance (see Acts 17:30; Rom. 7:7, 8; John 15:24).

And hath raised us up together, and made us sit together in heavenly places in Christ Jesus. (Eph. 2:4–6)

Not of works, lest any man should boast. For we are his workmanship, created in Christ Jesus unto good works, which God hath before ordained ["prepared in advance" (NIV)] that we should walk in them. (Eph. 2:9, 10)

Blessed be the God and Father of our Lord Jesus Christ, which according to his abundant mercy hath begotten us again unto a lively hope by the resurrection of Jesus Christ from the dead, *To an inheritance incorruptible, and undefiled, and that fadeth not away, reserved in heaven for you.* (1 Peter 1:3, 4)

If ye have heard of the dispensation [Greek definition: to manage, to administer, and/or the act of dispensing or dealing out, esp. as a steward or trustee of an estate] of the grace of God which is given me to you-ward. (Eph. 3:2)

For this cause also thank we God without ceasing, because, when ye received the word of God which ye heard of us, ye received it not as the word of men, but as it is in truth, the word of God, which effectually worketh also in you that believe. (1 Thess. 2:13)

And this I say, that the *covenant* [promise], that was confirmed before of God in Christ, the law, which was four hundred and thirty years after, cannot disannul, that it should make the *promise* of none effect. For if the inheritance be of the law, it is no more of promise: but God gave it to Abraham by *promise*. Wherefore then serveth the law? It was added [Greek definition: emphasized] because of transgressions, till the seed should come to whom the promise was made; and it was ordained by angels in the hand of a mediator. (Gal. 3:17–19)

In whom ye also trusted, after that ye heard the word of truth, the gospel of your salvation: in whom also after that ye believed, ye were sealed with that holy Spirit of promise, Which is the earnest of our inheritance until the redemption of the purchased possession, unto the praise of his glory. (Eph. 1:13, 14)

As soon as we *believe* the words of Christ, we have in very *deed* the peace which He has given.... They have made a profession of religion, but *real experience* means the *actual proving* of the power of the life of Christ. (E. J. Waggoner, *Waggoner on Romans*, pp. 93, 95)

All men have been bought with this infinite price. [**Title:**] By pouring the whole treasury of heaven into this world, by giving us in Christ all heaven, God has purchased the will, the affections, the mind, the soul, of every human being.…

Before He left His disciples, Christ "breathed on them, and saith unto them, Receive ye the Holy Ghost." John 20:22. Again He said, "Behold, I send the promise of My Father upon you." Luke 24:49. [**Possession:**] But not until after the ascension was the gift received in its fullness [at Pentecost]. Not until through faith and prayer the disciples had *surrendered* themselves fully for His working was the outpouring of the Spirit *received*. Then in a special sense [that is, in their experience] the goods of heaven were committed to the followers of Christ.… [**Title:**] The gifts are *already* ours *in Christ*, but their *actual possession* [that is, in our *experience*] depends upon our reception of the Spirit of God. (Ellen G. White, *Christ's Object Lessons*, pp. 326, 327)

"We are heirs of God and joint-heirs with Christ." That means that since we are joint-heirs with Christ, that Christ cannot enter into His inheritance without us. For if you and I are joint-heirs to an estate, we must have it together. You cannot enter into your inheritance before I enter and enjoy it with you. *Then whatever Christ is sharing now at the right hand of Father is for us.* He is at the right hand of God in the heavenly places and so we are quickened with Him and raised up and made to sit together in heavenly places with Christ Jesus.

By and by when Christ takes His own throne, we will take that too. In the first letter to the Corinthians it is written, "Eye hath not seen nor ear heard, neither have entered into the heart of man, the things which God hath prepared for them that love Him." 1 Corinthians 2:9. This has to do with the inheritance, but don't put it all off for the future. Go back a couple of verses—"We speak of the wisdom of God in a mystery, even the hidden wisdom, which God ordained before the world unto our glory. Which none of the princes of this world knew: for had they known it, they would not have crucified the Lord of glory." They might have known it, for read what follows in verse 10: "But God hath revealed them unto us by His Spirit."

It is something that God reveals to us now. We must not put it all off to the golden streets of the New Jerusalem, to the pearly gates, and the walls of jasper. And the only reason why we have not seen these things in the past is because the natural man cannot see them. [**Title:**] It is a precious thought and I want you to grasp it—that *everything that Christ has we have now.* Like David of old we can say, "The lines are fallen unto me in pleasant places; yea, I have a goodly heritage." Psalm 16:6. (E. J. Waggoner, *1891 General Conference Bulletin, No. 12*)

[**Title:**] If a room full of people be brilliantly lighted, each individual gets the benefit of all the light, just as much as though he were alone in the room. So the life of Christ lights every man that comes into the world. [**Possession:**] In every believing heart Christ dwells in His fullness. (E. J. Waggoner, *The Glad Tidings*, pp. 11, 12)

[**Title:**] "Christ redeemed us from the curse of the law" [from disobedience, which means the gift includes righteousness, a spiritual blessing as opposed to temporal (see Gal. 3:10)], from sin and death. This *He* has done by "being made a curse for us" [not by anything *we* did], and so we are freed from all necessity of sinning....

It is a full and complete [as opposed to "completed"] salvation that God has provided. *It awaits us as we come into the world.* And we do not relieve God of any burden by rejecting it, nor do we add to His labor by accepting it. [The benefits belong to us, just waiting for us to receive them. God does not have to do anything else to it to activate it, for it is a "done deal," so to speak. When we *believe*, we begin to *experience* the gift previously given and previously activated, like a debit card. If we choose not to believe, the gift just sits there waiting.] (E. J. Waggoner, *The Glad Tidings*, pp. 66, 67)

[**Title:**] It is true that, although a man may have all this in Jesus, [**Possession:**] he cannot profit by it [in his experience] without himself being a believer in Jesus. Take the man who does not believe in Jesus at all to-night. [**Title:**] Has not Christ made all the provision for him that he has for Elijah, who is in heaven to-night? And if this man wants to have Christ for his Saviour, if he wants provision made for all his sins, and salvation from all of them, does Christ have to do anything now, in order to provide for this man's sins, or to save him from them?—No; that is all done; he made all that provision for every man when he was in the flesh, [**Possession:**] and every man who believes in him receives this [in his experience] without there being [**Title:**] any need of any part of it being done over again. (A. T. Jones, *General Conference Bulletin 1895*, p. 268)

What This Means To Us

God gave us all things, including the Sabbath, in title by inheritance at Creation (Genesis 2:1–3). The Sabbath rest itself reminds us of God's ability, through the creative power of His word, to dispense from the trust fund when we believe. Our job is to rest in His power and completed work, not choosing our own way or running ahead of Him, but allowing Him to dispense His power to us as *He* sees we need it most.

The Three P's: Saved From What?

The Bible and the writings of Ellen White, A. T. Jones, and E. J. Waggoner all need to be understood and interpreted with three tenses in mind. What is the tense of the verb they are using? These represent the three phases of salvation. We will analyze some examples.

- **P1** – Christ saved us at the cross from the *penalty of sin*. (past)
- **P2** – Christ saves us now from the *power of sin* when we believe. (present)
- **P3** – Christ will save us in the future from the *presence of sin*. (future)

What This Means to Us

To avoid misunderstanding, we need to pay attention to the context of the statement. This will tell us which of the three phases the statement is expressing. Even the context of the verb tenses used can determine the subject of the statement. If written in the past tense, the statement probably applies to all people, not just to those who believe, unless the context clearly applies otherwise or is directed to a specific individual. The present and future tenses apply only to those who believe. Confusion here will result in apparent inconsistencies in these gospel writers.

> "In My name," Christ bade His disciples pray. In Christ's name His followers are to stand before God. Through the value of the sacrifice made for them, they are of value in the Lord's sight. Because of the imputed righteousness of Christ they are accounted precious. For Christ's sake the Lord pardons those that fear Him. He does not see in them the vileness of the sinner. He recognizes in them the likeness of His Son, in whom they believe.
>
> The Lord is disappointed when His people place a low estimate upon themselves. He desires His chosen heritage to value themselves according to the price *He* has placed upon them. God wanted them, else He would not have sent His Son on such an expensive errand to redeem them. He has a use for them, and He is well pleased when they make the very highest demands upon Him, that they may glorify His name. They may expect large things if they have faith in His promises. (Ellen G. White, *The Desire of Ages*, pp. 667, 668)

Now let's examine this example in light of the three P's as mentioned above:

- "'In My name,' Christ bade His disciples pray." P2 (*power of sin*) – Praying disciples are *believers.*
- "In Christ's name His followers are to stand before God." P2 (*power of sin*) – Followers are

believers. This is not to say that *only* Christ's followers stand before God. *All* who are in Christ stand before God favorably valued, which falls under P1. Those who *believe* take His family name, that is, "Christian."

- "Through the value of the sacrifice made for them, they are of value in the Lord's sight." P1 (*penalty of sin*) – Christ's sacrifice is *once*, for *all*, giving *all* people value in God's sight (Heb. 9:12).

- "Because of the imputed righteousness of Christ they are accounted precious." P1 (*penalty of sin*) – To impute means to *credit*, to arrange *title*[1]; this has been done for *everyone*. "With His own blood He has signed the emancipation papers [title] of the race" (Ellen G. White, *The Ministry of Healing*, p. 90).

- "For Christ's sake the Lord pardons those that fear Him." P2 (*power of sin*) – Those who fear God are believers. This is not to say that the Lord pardons *only* those who fear Him. He pardoned *everyone* before they knew what they were doing, which is P1. (See Pillar #1 and Luke 23:34.)

- "He does not see in them the vileness of the sinner." This is true while they remain "in Christ." "He recognizes in them the likeness of His Son, in whom they believe." P2 (*power of sin—again for believers*) – This is not saying that for *only* those who believe does God overlook in them the vileness of sin. *All* are "in Christ" before they know what they are doing, which is P1. (See Pillar #2, Acts 17:30, and Ephesians 1:3, 4.)

- "The Lord is disappointed when His people place a low estimate upon themselves. He desires His chosen heritage to value themselves according to the price He has placed upon them." P1 (*penalty of sin*) – The price paid was for all humanity. *All* have been *chosen*, but not all will believe.

- "God wanted them, else He would not have sent His Son on such an expensive errand to redeem them." P1 (*penalty of sin*) – The price paid was for all humanity.

- "He has a use for them, and He is well pleased when they make the very highest demands upon Him, that they may glorify His name." P2 (*power of sin*) – Only believers make demands upon God.

- "They may expect large things if they have faith in His promises." P2 (*power of sin*) – Faith is belief. The "large things" are the dispensation from the trust fund previously held only in *title* but now received in the *experience*.

To more fully understand this concept, let's look at another quote from Ellen G. White. This quote was taken from *This Day With God*.

> Oh, what soul hunger and longing had Christ to save that which was lost! The body crucified upon the cross did not detract from His divinity, His power of God to save through the human sacrifice, all who would accept His righteousness. In dying upon

---

1   To *impart* means to transmit, to arrange *substance*; this is done in the *experience* for those who *believe*, for faith is the *substance* of things expected (Heb. 11:1).

the cross, He transferred the guilt from the person of the transgressor to that of the divine Substitute through faith in Him as his personal Redeemer. The sins of a guilty world, which in figure are represented as "red as crimson," were imputed to the divine Surety…. (p. 236)

Let's examine this example in light of the three P's as mentioned above:

- "Oh, what soul hunger and longing had Christ to save that which was lost!" P1 (*penalty of sin*) – The whole world was lost.
- "The body crucified upon the cross did not detract from His divinity, His power of God to save through the human sacrifice, all who would accept His righteousness." P2 (*power of sin*) – Although not exactly the same as "believe," most people will identify "accept" with the believer.[2] This is not saying that God did not give salvation to all people. It merely states what happens to believers in the context of Christ's crucified body—that the fallen sinful human flesh that He took does not detract from His divinity.
- "In dying upon the cross, He transferred the guilt from the person of the transgressor to that of the divine Substitute through faith in Him as his personal Redeemer." P2 (*power of sin*) – Faith is belief.[3] To *transfer* is the same as transmit, to arrange substance, which is the definition of impart. The *substance* of the guilt is removed when we *believe*, which at that moment we realize (in our *experience*) we are free and have been free except that we did not know it (Rom. 10:17, "faith cometh by hearing"). Also, P1 in that what Christ did on the cross was for all people so that He gave (imputed) everyone the transfer of their guilt to Him, in title.
- "The sins of a guilty world, which in figure are represented as 'red as crimson,' were imputed to the divine Surety." P1 (*penalty of sin*) – The whole world is guilty. To *impute* is to *credit*, to arrange *title*.[4] This was done for the whole world. When one hears this good news and chooses to *believe*, what was his/hers only in *title*, now becomes part of his/her *experience*.

The Sabbath rest reminds us of the creative power of God's word to speak righteousness unto His people to save them from sin in all three phases, but especially the *power* of it. We need to rest from our *own* efforts[5] to do God's will or to complete God's promise of righteousness.

---

2   To "believe" means to have a heartfelt appreciation for and commitment to someone or something, a firm conviction. Substance (action) generally will follow in time. To "accept" means to have an intellectual assent to, indifference to, or to endure without protest; that may, or may not, lead to appreciation, commitment, or substantial results. In this passage, she is writing about our accepting the gift of Christ's righteousness, which we do through believing His word—His promise to us.

3   It's the same word in the Greek.

4   Note that Christ never committed sin, which means sin was never *imparted* to Him in *substance*. However, Christ did take *credit* for our sins, thus taking our penalty, the second death, for us.

5   Our *own* efforts are filthy rags (Isa. 64:6). Our own efforts to keep God's law are legalism at best.

God Is on Trial

The Bible refers to the great controversy theme in the legal terms of the judicial system. If we are willing to accept the metaphor, we can glean an understanding of the method God is using to resolve the great controversy issues with Satan. Let's look inside the courtroom. God is the defendant and judge, Satan is the plaintiff, we are God's witnesses, and the whole universe is the jury.

The hour of God's judgment has come. The issue is over God's character, who He is. The investigative judgment that is currently taking place in the heavenly sanctuary is determining who are God's witnesses and who will stand up and testify on His behalf as prophesied in the book of Revelation.

Satan, the plaintiff, wants to take the place of God. As he cross-examines the witnesses, he tries to get them to denounce God and speak against God's character. The whole universe (the jury) watches God's witnesses, His church, to determine the verdict in the great controversy between good and evil.

The work of the judge is to represent and deliver the defendant. This is how it is that God can be both the judge and the defendant. However, it is the jury that must be convinced that the plaintiff is wrong. The inhabitants of the whole universe are the ones who must be satisfied that sin must never rise again. Let's look at some scriptures.

The first four texts establish the work of the judge:

> Thou didst cause judgment to be heard from heaven; the earth feared, and was still, When God arose to judgment, to save all the meek of the earth. Selah. (Ps. 76:8, 9)

> Nevertheless the LORD raised up judges, which delivered them out of the hand of those that spoiled them. (Judges 2:16)

> The LORD therefore be judge, and judge between me and thee, and see, and plead my cause, and deliver me out of thine hand. (1 Sam. 24:15)

> Herein is our love made perfect, that we may have *boldness in the day of judgment*: because as he is [in heaven], so are we in this world. [Our deliverance is secure.] (1 John 4:17)

God's trial is announced in Revelation 14:6, 7: "And I saw another angel fly in the midst of heaven, having the everlasting gospel to preach unto them that dwell on the earth, and to every nation, and kindred, and tongue, and people, Saying with a loud voice, Fear God, and give glory to him; for the hour of His judgment is come: and worship him that made heaven, and earth, and the sea, and the fountains of waters."

Now the defendant begins His search for witnesses: "I tell you that he will avenge them speedily. Nevertheless when the Son of man cometh, shall he find faith on the earth? [He won't come until He does.]" (Luke 18:8).

The following quotes from Revelation 7 and 14 are actually descriptions of the subpoena process:

And after these things I saw four angels standing on the four corners of the earth, holding the four winds of the earth, that the wind should not blow on the earth, nor on the sea, nor on any tree. And I saw another angel ascending from the east, having the seal of the living God: and he cried with a loud voice to the four angels, to whom it was given to hurt the earth and the sea, Saying, Hurt not the earth, neither the sea, nor the trees, till we have sealed the servants of our God in their foreheads. And I heard the number of them which were sealed: and there were sealed an hundred and forty and four thousand of all the tribes of the children of Israel.

Of the tribe of Juda were sealed twelve thousand. Of the tribe of Reuben were sealed twelve thousand. Of the tribe of Gad were sealed twelve thousand. Of the tribe of Aser were sealed twelve thousand. Of the tribe of Nephthalim were sealed twelve thousand. Of the tribe of Manasses were sealed twelve thousand. Of the tribe of Simeon were sealed twelve thousand. Of the tribe of Levi were sealed twelve thousand. Of the tribe of Issachar were sealed twelve thousand. Of the tribe of Zabulon were sealed twelve thousand. Of the tribe of Joseph were sealed twelve thousand. Of the tribe of Benjamin were sealed twelve thousand.

After this I beheld, and, lo, a great multitude, which no man could number, of all nations, and kindreds, and people, and tongues, stood before the throne, and before the Lamb, clothed with white robes, and palms in their hands; And cried with a loud voice, saying, Salvation to our God which sitteth upon the throne, and unto the Lamb. And all the angels stood round about the throne, and about the elders and the four beasts, and fell before the throne on their faces, and worshipped God, Saying, Amen: Blessing, and glory, and wisdom, and thanksgiving, and honour, and power, and might, be unto our God for ever and ever. Amen.

And one of the elders answered, saying unto me, What are these which are arrayed in white robes? and whence came they? And I said unto him, Sir, thou knowest. And he said to me, These are they which came out of great tribulation, and have washed their robes, and made them white in the blood of the Lamb. Therefore are they before the throne of God, and serve him day and night in his temple: and he that sitteth on the throne shall dwell among them. They shall hunger no more, neither thirst any more; neither shall the sun light on them, nor any heat. For the Lamb which is in the midst of the throne shall feed them, and shall lead them unto living fountains of waters: and God shall wipe away all tears from their eyes. (Rev. 7:1–17)

And I looked, and, lo, a Lamb stood on the mount Sion, and with him an hundred forty and four thousand, having his Father's name written in their foreheads. And I heard a voice from heaven, as the voice of many waters, and as the voice of a great thunder: and I heard the voice of harpers harping with their harps: And they sung as it were a new song before the throne, and before the four beasts, and the elders: and no man could learn that song but the hundred and forty and four thousand, which were redeemed from the earth.

These are they which were not defiled with women; for they are virgins. These are they which follow the Lamb whithersoever he goeth. These were redeemed from among men, being the firstfruits unto God and to the Lamb. And in their mouth was found no guile: for they are without fault before the throne of God. And I saw another angel fly in the midst of heaven, having the everlasting gospel to preach unto them that dwell on the earth, and to every nation, and kindred, and tongue, and people, Saying with a loud voice, Fear God, and give glory to him; for the hour of his judgment is come: and worship him that made heaven, and earth, and the sea, and the fountains of waters. (Rev. 14:1–7)

And now for the jury:

And to make all men see what is the fellowship of the mystery, which from the beginning of the world hath been hid in God, who created all things by Jesus Christ: To the intent that now *unto the principalities and powers in heavenly places might be [made] known by the church* the manifold wisdom of God, According to the eternal purpose which he purposed in Christ Jesus our Lord. (Eph. 3:9–11)

Now for the trial itself:

Bring forth the blind people that have eyes, and the deaf that have ears. Let all the nations be gathered together, and let the people be assembled: who among them can declare this, and shew us former things? let them bring forth their witnesses, that they may be justified: or let them hear, and say, It is truth. Ye are my witnesses, saith the LORD, and my servant whom I have chosen: that ye may know and believe me, and understand that I am he: before me there was no God formed, neither shall there be after me. I, even I, am the LORD; and beside me there is no saviour. I have declared, and have saved, and I have shewed, when there was no strange god among you: therefore ye are my witnesses, saith the LORD, that I am God. Yea, before the day was I am he; and there is none that can deliver out of my hand: I will work, and who shall let it? Thus saith the LORD, your redeemer, the Holy One of Israel; For your sake I have sent to Babylon, and have brought down all their nobles, and the Chaldeans, whose cry is in the ships. (Isa. 43:8–14)

Now let's look at the plaintiff. He has a claim. Let's see what it is:

How art thou fallen from heaven, O Lucifer, son of the morning! how art thou cut down to the ground, which didst weaken the nations! For thou hast said in thine heart, I will ascend into heaven, I will exalt my throne above the stars [angels] of God: I will sit also upon the mount of the congregation, in the sides of the north [a reference to God's dwelling place]: I will ascend above the heights of the clouds; *I will be like the most High.* (Isa. 14:12–14)

One of the plaintiff's tasks is to cross-examine the witnesses. Let's see how this works out. Note here that Satan is trying to attend this meeting as the representative from earth. God's response is to not admit him, using Job's loyalty to God as his reason:

Now there was a day when the sons of God came to present themselves before the LORD, and Satan came also among them. And the LORD said unto Satan, Whence comest thou? Then Satan answered the LORD, and said, From going to and fro in the earth, and from walking up and down in it. [Notice that Satan is claiming to represent planet Earth at this meeting, but the LORD denies it.] And the LORD said unto Satan, Hast thou considered my servant Job, that there is none like him in the earth, a perfect and an upright man, one that feareth God, and escheweth evil? [Now comes the cross-examination.] Then Satan answered the LORD, and said, Doth Job fear God for nought? Hast not thou made an hedge about him, and about his house, and about all that he hath on every side? thou hast blessed the work of his hands, and his substance is increased in the land. [That is, Job is not a true witness.] But put forth thine hand now, and touch all that he hath, and he will curse thee to thy face. And the LORD said unto Satan, Behold, all that he hath is in thy power; only upon himself put not forth thine hand. So Satan went forth from the presence of the LORD. (Job 1:6–12)

Other writers also comment on God's trial:

Satan had pointed to Adam's sin as proof that God's law was unjust, and could not be obeyed. *In our humanity, Christ was to redeem Adam's failure....* For four thousand years the race had been decreasing in physical strength, in mental power, and in moral worth; and Christ took upon Him the infirmities of *degenerate* humanity. Only thus could He rescue man from the lowest depths of his degradation. [Only thus could He *qualify* to represent the human race.] (Ellen G. White, *The Desire of Ages*, p. 117)

God is Himself on trial before the universe and Satan and evil men have always charged Him with being unjust and arbitrary, but in the judgment all the universe will say, "Just and true are thy ways, thou King of saints." (E. J. Waggoner, *General Conference Bulletin, 1891*, no. 3, p. 1.4)

He [Christ] came into the world to demonstrate the unrighteousness of that argument that Satan was presenting in the courts of God, as the prosecuting attorney from this country. That is the thought; it is legal all the way through. ... And he conquered, and thus became, by right, the head of this dominion again and of all who will be redeemed from it, and of the redemption of the dominion itself.

And now that word also in the Greek which says that the accuser of our brethren "is cast down," conveys the idea of a prosecuting attorney, who comes into court, but he has no case any more; he is repudiated; he has no place for argument. Why?—because now we have an Advocate in the court, Jesus Christ the righteous. Yes; thank the Lord! (A. T. Jones, *General Conference Bulletin, 1895*, p. 448)

What This Means to Us

In virtually every case, the word "deliverance" can be substituted for the word "judgment" because the work of the judge is to deliver the defendant. Only if the judge fails, or the defendant repudiates the work of the judge, does the defendant receive the penalty.[1] As long as the defendant allows the heavenly Judge to represent him/her, the defendant is acquitted, because of His all-powerful creative word. When we make the substitution of these two words, the result is much more encouraging as well as being truth. The judge is our Deliverer! He delivers from all three phases of sin through the power of His word *alone*.

In John 5:30, Jesus said, "I can of mine own self do nothing: as I hear, I judge: and my judgment is just." The word "just" means righteous. That's where we get our word "justification" from. Righteousness by faith and justification by faith say the same thing. Jesus judges only righteousness. His judgment on us, by His word only, is "be ye therefore perfect" and "go and sin no more." His word has inherent

---

1   For an earthly judge this can happen either through the imperfection of the judge or from overwhelming and incontrovertible evidence against the defendant. For the heavenly Judge, this can happen only through the defendant's own unbelief (John 3:18).

within it the power to create what it says.

Take a look at the following verses:

- Isaiah 26:9 – God's judgments bring righteousness.
- Isaiah 1:21 – Righteousness and judgment coexist.
- Isaiah 45:19 – God speaks (or brings forth) righteousness. He can only declare things that are right because His word has inherent within it the power to create what it says. (This would be as true in passing judgment as at any other time.)
- John 12:31, 32 – Judgment (deliverance) has already been passed when Christ died on the cross. You *are* delivered from sin!

The Sabbath rest reminds us of who God is—Creator with His all-powerful inherently creative word—and what He can do in fallen sinful human flesh—the flesh He took upon Himself, which is the same flesh that you and I have because of Adam's sin. This confirms that He can and does prove what He can do in your fallen sinful human flesh, and my fallen sinful human flesh, and of the next person, and of every person who will allow Him to dwell in them through the power of the Holy Spirit, all through His spoken word. Resting in God's all-powerful creative spoken, written, and living Word is true righteousness by faith. It demonstrates who God is. It answers the charge of the plaintiff in God's trial. When we observe the Sabbath as God ordained it, we are witnesses all week long, testifying to the authority of our God who is on trial.

The Work in the Sanctuary: The Earthly Illustrates the Heavenly

The earthly sanctuary was modeled after the heavenly sanctuary, and the various sacrifices and feasts all pointed forward to Christ's mission on earth and the redemptive work that He is performing in the heavenly sanctuary.

And let them make me a sanctuary; that I may dwell among them. According to all that I shew thee, after the pattern of the tabernacle, and the pattern of all the instruments thereof, even so shall ye make it. (Exod. 25:8, 9)

Included in this pattern are the daily, weekly, and annual services (including the seven feasts). Part of the annual services was the Day of Atonement, the annual cleansing of the earthly sanctuary by the high priest. This, too, was made after the pattern of the heavenly cleansing of the sanctuary of the sins of God's people.[1]

Who serve unto the example and shadow of heavenly things, as Moses was admonished of God when he was about to make the tabernacle: for, See, saith he, that thou make all things according to the pattern shewed to thee in the mount. (Heb. 8:5)

The holy places made with hands were to be "figures of the true," "patterns of things in the heavens" (Hebrews 9:24, 23)—a miniature representation of the heavenly temple where Christ, our great High Priest, after offering His life as a sacrifice, was to minister in the sinner's behalf. God presented before Moses in the mount a view of the heavenly sanctuary, and commanded him to make all things according to the pattern shown him. (Ellen G. White, *Patriarchs and Prophets*, p. 343)

The cleansing of the sanctuary [Daniel 8:14] and the finishing of the mystery of God [Revelation 10:7] are identical as to time; and are also so closely related as to be practically identical in character and event.

---

1   The Day of Atonement itself, being a pattern of heavenly things, has its antitypical fulfillment in the preparation of God's people for the eradication of sin and the coming of Christ to set up His everlasting and eternal kingdom. A study of the typical day illustrates the activities in the antitypical day of which there are four reforms God is doing during that time: health reform, dress reform, Sabbath reform, and gospel reform, which is another subject for another time.

In the "figure of the true" in the sanctuary service made visible, the round of service was completed annually, and the *cleansing of the sanctuary* was the *finishing* of that figurative and annual service. And this cleansing of the sanctuary was the taking out of and away from the sanctuary all "the uncleanness of the children of Israel" "because of their transgression in all their sins," which, by the ministry of the priesthood in the sanctuary, had been brought into the sanctuary during the service of the year.

The finishing of this work of the sanctuary and for the sanctuary was, likewise, the finishing of the work *for the people*. For in that day of the cleansing of the sanctuary, which was the day of atonement, whosoever of the people did not by searching of heart, confession, and putting away of sin, take part in the service of the cleansing of the sanctuary was cut off forever. Thus the cleansing of the sanctuary extended to *the people*, and included *the people*, as truly as it did the sanctuary itself. And whosoever of the people was not included in the cleansing of the sanctuary, and was not *himself cleansed*, equally with the sanctuary, from all iniquity and transgression and sin, was cut off forever. Lev. 16:15–19, 29–34; 23:27–32.

And this was all "a figure for the time then present." That sanctuary, sacrifice, priesthood, and ministry was a figure of *the true*, which is the sanctuary, sacrifice, priesthood, and ministry of Christ. And that *cleansing* of the sanctuary was a figure of the true, which is the cleansing of the sanctuary and the true tabernacle which the Lord pitched and not man, from all the uncleanness of the believers in Jesus because of all their transgressions in all their sins. And the time of this cleansing of the true is declared in the words of the Wonderful Numberer to be "unto two thousand and three hundred days, then shall the sanctuary be cleansed," which is the sanctuary of Christ in A.D. 1844.[2]

And, indeed, the sanctuary of which Christ is the High Priest is the only one that could possibly be cleansed in 1844, because it is the only one that there is. (A. T. Jones, *The Consecrated Way to Christian Perfection*, pp. 113, 114, emphasis original)

What This Means to Us

The earthly and heavenly sanctuaries illustrate that God's forgiveness is redemptive. The main part of being "a miniature representation of the heavenly temple where Christ, our great High Priest, ... was to minister in the sinner's behalf" (*Patriarchs and Prophets*, p. 343) was the work of the earthly high

---

2   Daniel 8:14 reveals this time prophecy. From the autumn of 457 BC (the command that successfully resulted in the rebuilding of Jerusalem) to the autumn of 1844 (allowing for no year 0) is 2300 years. From the autumn of AD 27 (the baptism of Christ and the beginning of His ministry) to the spring of AD 31 at Passover (the death of Christ) is the halfway point of the final seven-year period of the 490 years of the final Jewish era that ended when the Jews began wholesale persecution of the Christians at the stoning of Stephen in the autumn of AD 34. During this week Christ "confirmed the covenant with many" and "caused the sacrifice and the oblation to cease," thus ending the ministry of the earthly sanctuary, as prophesied in Daniel 9:27. (See Daniel 8 and 9 and Acts 6–8.)

priest who annually entered the Most Holy Place of the earthly sanctuary to remove the sins of the people. Therefore, God not only pardons our sin, but He removes the sin and the guilt. He did this—in title, as a trust—on the cross, and He is doing this now as His work in the Most Holy Place of the heavenly sanctuary dispensing the assets of the trust and cleansing the sanctuary of the sins of the people (in their experience), thus preparing a people for His vindication in His trial and for His coming to receive His inheritance. Let us be a part of this glorious work.

- 1 John 1:9 – "God is faithful and just to forgive us … and to cleanse us."
- Zechariah 3:1-5 – The old filthy garments are removed first.
- John 8:11 – "Neither do I condemn thee: go, and sin no more."

God's ideal for His children is higher than the highest human thought can reach. "Be ye therefore perfect, even as your Father which is in heaven is perfect." *This command is a promise. The plan of redemption contemplates our complete recovery from the power of Satan. Christ always separates the contrite soul from sin.* He came to destroy the works of the devil, and He has made provision that the Holy Spirit shall be imparted to every repentant soul, to keep him from sinning. (Ellen G. White, *The Desire of Ages*, p. 311)

The religion of Christ means more than the forgiveness of sin; it means taking away our sins, and filling the vacuum with the graces of the Holy Spirit. It means divine illumination, rejoicing in God. It means a heart emptied of self, and blessed with the abiding presence of Christ. When Christ reigns in the soul, there is purity, freedom from sin. The glory, the fullness, the completeness of the gospel plan is fulfilled in the life. The acceptance of the Saviour brings a glow of perfect peace, perfect love, perfect assurance. The beauty and fragrance of the character of Christ revealed in the life testifies that God has indeed sent His Son into the world to be its Saviour. (Ellen G. White, *Christ's Object Lessons*, pp. 419, 420)

Thus the services of the sanctuary, in the offering of the sacrifices and the ministering of the priests, and of the high priests alone, was for the making of atonement, and for the forgiveness and *sending away of the sins of the people*. Because of the sin and guilt, because of their having "done somewhat against any of the commandments of the Lord concerning things which should not be done," atonement must be made and forgiveness obtained. Atonement is literally at-one-ment. The sin and the guilt had separated them from God. By these services they were made at-one with God. Forgive is literally give-for. To forgive sin is to give for sin. Forgiveness of sin comes alone from God. What does God give, what has He given, for sin? He gave Christ, and Christ "gave himself for our sins." Gal. 1:4; Eph. 2:12–16; Rom. 5:8–11. (A. T. Jones, *The Consecrated Way to Christian Perfection*, pp. 66, 67)

When sin is pointed out to you, say, "I would rather have Christ than that." And let it go. [Congregation: "Amen."] Just tell the Lord, "Lord, I make the choice now; I make the trade; I make thee my choice; it is gone, and I have something better." Thank the Lord! Then where in the world is the opportunity for any of us to get discouraged over our sins?

Now some of the brethren here have done that very thing. They came here free; but the Spirit of God brought up something they never saw before. The Spirit of God went deeper than it ever went before, and revealed things they never saw before; and then, instead of thanking the Lord that that was so, and letting the whole wicked business go, and thanking the Lord they had ever so much more of Him than they ever had before, they began to get discouraged....

If the Lord has brought up sins to us that we never thought of before, that only shows that he is going down to the depths, and he will reach the bottom at last; and when he finds the last thing that is unclean or impure, that is out of harmony with his will, and brings that up, and shows that to us, and we say, "I would rather have the Lord than that,"—then the work is complete, and the seal of the living God can be fixed upon that character....

Which would you rather, have the completeness, the perfect fulness, of Jesus Christ, or have less than that, with some of your sins covered up that you never know of? [Congregation: "His fulness."] But don't you see, the Testimonies have told us that if there be stains of sin there, we cannot have the seal of God. How in the world can that seal of God, which is the impress of his perfect character revealed in us, be put upon us when there are sins about us? He cannot put the seal, the impress of his perfect character, upon us until he sees it there. And so he has got to dig down to the deep places we never dreamed of, because we cannot understand our hearts. But the Lord knows the heart. He tries the conscience. He will cleanse the heart, and bring up the last vestige of wickedness. Let Him go on, brethren; let him keep on his searching work. (A. T. Jones, *General Conference Bulletin 1893*, p. 404)

The furniture in the sanctuary represents God's redemptive work. The table with its two stacks of shewbread represents Christ as the nourishing Bread of Life[3] and the throne of both the Father and Son during the first-apartment ministry. The altar (sometimes called "table") of incense represents the merits of Christ and also the prayers of God's people ascending into the Most Holy Place. The candlestick of everlasting oil and fire represents Christ as the illuminating light of the world and also God as a sanctifying consuming fire that cleanses sin, causing God's people to have a holy influence upon others. All of this is the *daily* ministration of the High Priest in the holy place first-apartment ministry of the heavenly sanctuary and represents the daily experience of God's people.

---

3   We receive nourishment through the study of God's Word.

The annual ministration took place in the Most Holy Place (the second-apartment ministry). It includes the ark of the covenant with the tables of the law and the mercy seat and represents the closing work of the cleansing of the heavenly sanctuary—the preparation of God's people for the coming of Christ. It also represents the throne of God during this period of the second-apartment ministry.

(For a more in-depth discussion of the furniture, including the cleansing fire, please see the Appendix).

The Sabbath reminds us of the power of God's creative word to remove sin from His people in the last days so that the heavenly sanctuary can be cleansed. Then Christ can come to receive His inheritance (see Gal. 3:16)!

In conclusion, I would like to quote one of my favorite Bible authors: "Such was the service performed 'unto the example and shadow of heavenly things.' And what was done in type in the ministration of the earthly sanctuary is done in reality in the ministration of the heavenly sanctuary. After His ascension our Saviour began His work as our high priest. Says Paul: 'Christ is not entered into the holy places made with hands, which are the figures of the true; but into heaven itself, now to appear in the presence of God for us.' Hebrews 9:24" (Ellen G. White, *The Great Controversy*, p. 420).

The Reward of Heaven

God is trying to get you into heaven, not keep you out. He paid an infinite price to give you salvation, for Jesus Christ Himself is the Price. He is not going to leave you at the checkout counter.

What? know ye not that your body is the temple of the Holy Ghost which is in you, which ye have of God, and ye are not your own? For ye are bought with a price: therefore glorify God in your body, and in your spirit, which are God's. (1 Cor. 6:19, 20)

Let this mind be in you, which was also in Christ Jesus: Who, being in the form of God, thought it not robbery to be equal with God: But made himself of no reputation, and took upon him the form of a servant, and was made in the likeness of men: And being found in fashion as a man, he humbled himself, and became obedient unto death, even the death of the cross. (Phil. 2:5–8)

For ye know the grace of our Lord Jesus Christ, that, though he was rich, yet for your sakes he became poor, that ye through his poverty might be rich. (2 Cor. 8:9)

Fear not, little flock; for it is your Father's good pleasure to *give* you the kingdom. (Luke 12:32)

"In My name," Christ bade His disciples pray. In Christ's name His followers are to stand before God. Through the value of the sacrifice made for them, they are of value in the Lord's sight. Because of the *imputed* righteousness of Christ they are *accounted* precious [not by anything *they* did]….

The Lord is disappointed when His people place a low estimate upon themselves. He desires His chosen heritage to value themselves according to the price He has placed upon them. God wanted them, else He would not have sent His Son on such an expensive errand to redeem them. He has a use for them, and He is well pleased when they make the very highest demands upon Him, that they may glorify His name. They may expect large things if they have faith in His promises. (Ellen G. White, *The Desire of Ages*, pp. 667, 668)

Many people hesitate to make a start to serve the Lord, because they fear that God will not accept them; …

I reply by another question: Will a man receive that which he has bought? If you go to the store and make a purchase, will you receive the goods when they are delivered?… The fact that you bought the goods and paid your money for them is sufficient proof, not only that you are *willing*, but that you are *anxious*, to receive them.…

Now let us apply this simple, natural illustration to the case of the sinner coming to Christ.… He has bought us.…

The price that was paid for us was His own blood—His life.… He "gave himself for us." Titus 2:14.…

He bought not a certain class, but the whole world of sinners. "For God so loved the world, that he gave his only-begotten Son." John 3:16. Jesus said, "The bread that I will give is my flesh, which I will give for the life of the world." John 6:51. "For when we were yet without strength, in due time Christ died for the ungodly." "God commendeth his love toward us, in that, while we were yet sinners, Christ died for us." Romans 5:6, 8.…

"But I am not worthy." That means that you are not worth the price paid and therefore you fear to come lest Christ will repudiate the purchase. Now you might have some fear on that score if the bargain were not sealed and the price were not already paid.…

But, further, you have nothing to do with the question of worth.… He made the purchase with his eyes [wide] open, and He knew the exact value of that which He bought. He is not at all disappointed when you come to Him and He finds that you are worthless. You have not to worry over the question of worth. If He, with His perfect knowledge of the case, was satisfied to make the bargain, you should be the last one to complain.

For, most wonderful truth of all, He bought you for the very *reason* that you were not worthy. His practiced eye saw in you great possibilities, and He bought you, not for what you were then or are now worth, but for what He could *make* of you.… We have no righteousness, therefore He bought us, "that we might be *made* the righteousness of God in Him" [2 Cor. 5:21]. (E. J. Waggoner, *Christ and His Righteousness*, pp. 69–73)

The Sabbath reminds us of the free and abundant entrance into the kingdom that God has provided, for when He was finished with Creation, He *rested* from the work that he had proclaimed "very good." It reminds us that *we* can rest in God's work also. Therefore, God takes us by the hand and tugs gently but firmly, saying, "Come on. Come on! Let's go to heaven together. Shall we?" The only way we can be lost is through unbelief. The only way we can be lost is by calling God a liar and refusing the gift so freely given. It is easy to be saved; it is hard to be lost .

Jesus said, "Come unto me, all ye that labour and are heavy laden, and I will give you rest" (Matt. 11:28). He promises that His "yoke" is easy and His burden light (verse 30). As Saul discovered, "it is hard … to kick against the pricks" (Acts 9:5). Through his encounter on the road to Damascus, Saul, who became Paul, found out how easy it is to be saved (Acts. 26:14).

> Yet do not therefore conclude that the upward path is the hard and the downward road the easy way. All along the road that leads to death there are pains and penalties, there are sorrows and disappointments, there are warnings *not* to go on. God's love has made it hard for the heedless and headstrong to destroy themselves. (Ellen G. White, *Thoughts from the Mount of Blessing*, p 139)

When we understand and appreciate how good the good news really is, the pressure is off and we are free—in deed. Think about it.

"I Jesus have sent mine angel to testify unto you these things in the churches. I am the root and the offspring of David, and the bright and morning star. And the Spirit and the bride say, Come. And let him that heareth say, Come. And let him that is athirst come. And whosoever will, let him take the water of life freely" (Rev. 22:16, 17). Amen.

The Outer Court (open to the public)

The Inner Court (Jews only for the daily ministrations of taking care of sins of the people)

Each day sinners brought animal sacrifices to the sanctuary. This pointed forward to Christ as the true Lamb of God who was sacrificed for our sins.

The **altar of sacrifice** was where the sinner killed the animal himself. The sacrifice was also burned on the altar.

Veil
*

The **laver** was for washing. The priests washed their hands and feet before taking part in any portion of the sacred sanctuary services.

The Sanctuary (priests only)

The Holy Place
(first apartment):
This is where the daily ministration took place.

The **table of shewbread** with two stacks of bread represents Christ as our Bread of Life. It also symbolized the throne of the Father and the Son during the daily ministration.

The **seven candlesticks** point to Christ as the Light of the World. It also symbolized the work of the Holy Spirit (oil) cleansing sin and refining the character (fire).

The Most Holy Place
(second apartment):
The annual cleansing of the sanctuary by the high priest took place in this area.

The **altar of incense** represents the merits of Christ. It also represents the prayers of the people ascending to the throne of God in the Most Holy Place.

Veil
*

Ark of the Covenant[1]

The main throne room: On top of the ark was the mercy seat with the two covering cherubs. Inside the ark were the two stone tablets upon which God wrote the ten commandments with His own finger, the golden pot of manna, and Aaron's rod that budded. Outside the ark were the golden censor and the Pentateuch.

N

not to scale

1 - The exact position of the furniture within the room is not precisely known
* - Two veils (Heb. 9:3)

The Outer Court (open to the public)

Appendix

The Furniture in the Sanctuary

What This Means to Us

The furniture in the sanctuary represents God's redemptive work. As mentioned in Pillar #6, the table with its two stacks of shewbread represents Christ as the nourishing Bread of Life and the throne of both the Father and Son during the first-apartment ministry. The altar (sometimes called "table") of incense represents the merits of Christ and also the prayers of God's people ascending into the Most Holy Place. The candlestick of everlasting oil and fire represents Christ as the illuminating light of the world and also God as a sanctifying consuming fire that cleanses sin, causing God's people to have a holy influence upon others. All of this is the *daily* ministration of the High Priest in the holy place first-apartment ministry of the heavenly sanctuary and represents the daily experience of God's people.

The annual ministration took place in the Most Holy Place (the second-apartment ministry). It includes the ark of the covenant with the tables of the law and the mercy seat and represents the closing work of the cleansing of the heavenly sanctuary—the preparation of God's people for the coming of Christ. It also represents the throne of God during this period of the second-apartment ministry.

> In the holy place was the candlestick, on the south,[1] with its seven lamps giving light to the sanctuary both by day and by night; on the north[2] stood the table of shewbread; and before the veil separating the holy from the most holy was the golden altar of incense, from which the cloud of fragrance, with the prayers of Israel, was daily ascending before God.
>
> In the most holy place stood the ark, a chest of precious wood overlaid with gold, the depository of the two tables of stone upon which God had inscribed the law of Ten Commandments. Above the ark, and forming the cover to the sacred chest, was the mercy seat, a magnificent piece of workmanship, surmounted by two cherubim, one at each end, and all wrought of solid gold. In this apartment the divine presence was manifested in the cloud of glory between the cherubim. (Ellen G. White, *The Great Controversy*, p. 412)

Now let's look at each piece of furniture in the light of the earthly type and heavenly antitype:

---

1   The entrance faced east. It is said that when Christ comes again it will be from the east (Isa. 41:25; Matt. 24:27).

2   God's throne is considered to reside in the north, which is on the right (honor/action) side of the sanctuary as you go in (Ps. 48:1, 2; Isa. 14:13; 41:25).

The table of shewbread
- Earthly type
  — Shewbread in two stacks (Lev. 24:5–7).
- Heavenly antitype
  — Christ is the Bread of Life (John 6:26–33).

Regarding the heavenly antitype, I offer the following:

> I saw a throne, and on it sat the Father and the Son. I gazed on Jesus' countenance and admired His lovely person. The Father's person I could not behold, for a cloud of glorious light covered Him. I asked Jesus if His Father had a form like Himself. He said He had, but I could not behold it, for said He, "If you should once behold the glory of His person, you would cease to exist."…
>
> I saw the Father rise from the throne, and in a flaming chariot go into the holy of holies within the veil, and sit down.… Then a cloudy chariot, with wheels like flaming fire, surrounded by angels, came to where Jesus was. He stepped into the chariot and was borne to the holiest, where the Father sat. There I beheld Jesus, a great High Priest, standing before the Father. (Ellen G. White, *Early Writings*, pp. 54, 55)

The altar of incense
- Earthly type
  — The altar of incense was built to exact specifications (Exod. 30:1–10)
  — The incense itself was to burn at all times (Exod. 30:34, 35)
- Heavenly antitype
  — "And another angel came and stood at the altar, having a golden censer; and there was given unto him much incense, that he should offer it with the prayers of all saints upon the golden altar which was before the throne. And the smoke of the incense, which came with the prayers of the saints, ascended up before God out of the angel's hand" (Rev. 8:3, 4).

Regarding the heavenly antitype:

> By His spotless life, His obedience, His death on the cross of Calvary, Christ interceded for the lost race. And now, not as a mere petitioner does the Captain of our salvation intercede for us, but as a Conqueror claiming His victory. His offering is complete, and as our Intercessor He executes His self-appointed work, holding before God the censer containing His own spotless merits and the prayers, confessions, and thanksgiving of His people. Perfumed with the fragrance of His righteousness, these ascend to God as a sweet savor. The offering is wholly acceptable, and pardon covers all transgression. (Ellen G. White, *Christ's Object Lessons*, p. 156)

The candlestick

- Earthly type
  — Candlestick of oil and fire and light (Exod. 25:31–40)
- Heavenly antitype
  — The light represents Christ who is the Light of the world (John 8:12).
  — The olive oil represents the work of the Holy Spirit applying the grace of God, the refining merits of Christ (Zech. 4:1–6).
  — The fire represents God, particularly that aspect of His work that refines and cleanses us from sin (Zech. 13:1, 9; Deut. 4:24).
  — The lake of fire is not for human beings but is for the devil and his angels (Matt. 25:41).

Regarding the heavenly antitype:

The continued communication of the Holy Spirit to the church is represented by the prophet Zechariah under another figure, which contains a wonderful lesson of encouragement for us…. [Quotes from Zechariah 4.]…

From the two olive trees, the golden oil was emptied through golden pipes into the bowl of the candlestick and thence into the golden lamps that gave light to the sanctuary. So from the holy ones that stand in God's presence, His Spirit is imparted to human instrumentalities that are consecrated to His service. The mission of the two anointed ones is to communicate light and power to God's people. It is to receive blessing for us that they stand in God's presence. As the olive trees empty themselves into the golden pipes, so the heavenly messengers seek to communicate all that they receive from God. The whole heavenly treasure [P1 – in trust, in title] awaits our demand and reception [P2 – the dispensation]; and as we receive the blessing, we in our turn are to impart it. Thus it is that the holy lamps are fed, and the church becomes a light bearer in the world.

This is the work that the Lord would have every soul prepared to do at this time, when the four angels are holding the four winds, that they shall not blow until the servants of God are sealed in their foreheads….

To us is committed the arduous, but happy, glorious work of revealing Christ to those who are in darkness. We are called to proclaim the *special truths for this time* [Remember: this was written in 1897.]. For all this the outpouring of the Spirit is essential. We should pray for it. The Lord expects us to ask Him. (Ellen G. White, *Testimonies to Ministers and Gospel Workers,* pp. 509–512)

"Who may abide the day of his coming? Who shall stand when he appeareth? for he is like a *refiner's* FIRE." Good. Then when I meet him *now*, in the consuming fire that He is, I meet him in a fire that is refining, that purifies. "And he shall sit as a refiner and purifier of silver: and he shall purify the sons of Levi, and purge them as gold and silver, that they may offer unto the Lord an offering in righteousness." *That* is separation from sin; that is purification from sin. And that sets us where we offer an offering unto the Lord in righteousness: we become the servants of righteousness unto holiness, that we may meet the Lord. So, then, bless the Lord that he is a consuming fire,—that he is as a refiner's fire.

Look again at that expression in Revelation: "His eyes were as a flame of fire." In that day his eyes will rest upon each one of us, and he will look clear through us. When his eyes are as a flame of fire, and those eyes in that great day rest upon every one of us, and look clear through us, what will that look do for every one who is wrapped up, body and soul, in sin?—It will consume the sin, and the sinner with it; because he would not be separated from the sin. And *today*, just now, those eyes are the same that they will be in *that* day. Today his eyes are as a flame of fire; and "all things are naked and opened unto the eyes of him with whom we have to do." Very good, then. As all things are naked and opened unto the eyes of him with whom we have to do, whether we *will have* to do with Him or not, why not accept the fact, choose to have it so, and on our part open up everything to the eyes of him with whom we have to do? And having opened up the life thus to him, to the flaming fire of the glory of his shining eyes, what will that do?—Those eyes of living flame will look clear through us, and will consume away all the sin, and all the dross; and will refine us so that He shall see in us the image of himself. (A. T. Jones, *Our God is a Consuming Fire,* pp. 16–18, emphasis original)

All the Scripture is founded upon this thought,—that it is not against the *person*, but against the *thing to which the person has fastened himself*, that the wrath of God comes. Then as the Lord executes vengeance primarily only against sin, as his wrath is only against ungodliness and unrighteousness, and he has done everything he could to get the people to separate from sin, then in that burning day when he comes, and reveals himself to the world, and the world sees him as he is, it will still be only sin against which he will execute vengeance. (A. T. Jones, *Our God is a Consuming Fire,* p. 8, emphasis original)

However, in that day, as in all other days, it is not upon men *themselves* that God's wrath is visited; but upon the *sins* of men, and upon *men only* as they are identified with their *sins*. "For the wrath of God is revealed from heaven," not against all ungodly men, not against all unrighteous men, but "against all ungodli*ness* and unrigh-teous*ness* of men." Rom. 1:18. And only as the man clings to his ungodliness, only as he holds down the truth in unrighteousness, shall it be that the wrath of God will be revealed from heaven against him: and even then not against *him* primarily, but against the sin to which he clings, and will not leave. And as he has thus made his choice, clinging fast to his choice, he must take the consequences of his choice, when his choice shall have reached its ultimate. So it is written, and I read it again, "The wrath of God is revealed from heaven against all ungodliness and unrighteousness of men, who hold the truth [who hold down, who press back the truth] in unrighteousness." (A. T. Jones, *Our God is a Consuming Fire,* pp. 2, 3, emphasis original)

The finishing of the mystery of God is the ending of the work of the gospel. And the ending of the work of the gospel is, *first, the taking away of all vestige of sin* and the bringing in of everlasting righteousness—Christ fully formed—within each believer, God alone manifest in the flesh of each believer in Jesus; and, *secondly,* on the other hand, the work of the gospel being finished means only the destruction of all who then shall not have received the gospel (2 Thess. 1:7-10): for it is not the way of the Lord to continue men in life when the only possible use they will make of life is to heap up more misery for themselves. (A. T. Jones, *The Consecrated Way to Christian Perfection*, pp. 117, 118, emphasis original)

The Ark of the Covenant (the place on which God establishes His throne)
- Earthly type
  — The Most Holy Place is described in Exodus 25:10–22.
- Heavenly antitype
  — God's throne room is described in Revelation 4 and 5.

Such was the service performed "unto the example and shadow of heavenly things." And what was done in *type* in the ministration of the earthly sanctuary is done in *reality* in the ministration of the heavenly sanctuary. After His ascension our Saviour began His work as our high priest. Says Paul: "Christ is not entered into the holy places made with hands, which are the figures of the true; but into heaven itself, now to appear in the presence of God for us." Hebrews 9:24. (Ellen G. White, *The Great Controversy*, p. 420)

Index

Y

We invite you to view the complete
selection of titles we publish at:

www.TEACHServices.com

Scan with your mobile
device to go directly
to our website.

Please write or email us your praises, reactions, or
thoughts about this or any other book we publish at:

TEACH Services, Inc.
P U B L I S H I N G
www.TEACHServices.com • (800) 367-1844

P.O. Box 954
Ringgold, GA 30736

info@TEACHServices.com

TEACH Services, Inc., titles may be purchased in bulk for
educational, business, fund-raising, or sales promotional use.
For information, please e-mail:

BulkSales@TEACHServices.com

Finally, if you are interested in seeing
your own book in print, please contact us at

publishing@TEACHServices.com

We would be happy to review your manuscript for free.

www.ingramcontent.com/pod-product-compliance
Lightning Source LLC
Chambersburg PA
CBHW080536090426
42733CB00015B/2605